# THE
# FUNNIEST
# SPURS
# QUOTES...
# EVER!

# About the author

Gordon Law is a freelance journalist and editor who has previously covered football for the *South London Press*, the *Premier League*, *Virgin Media* and a number of English national newspapers and magazines. He has also written several books on the beautiful game.

# THE
# FUNNIEST
# SPURS
# QUOTES...
# EVER!

## by Gordon Law

Printed in the United States of America
ISBN-13: 978-1540404220
ISBN-10: 1540404226

Photos courtesy of: Mitch Gunn/Shutterstock.com and Ramzi
Musallam.

# Contents

# Introduction

Legendary Tottenham Hotspur manager Bill Nicholson once said: "I prefer players not to be too good or too clever at other things. It means they concentrate on football."

It's no wonder then that footballers – who it's often said have their brains in their feet – are able to provide such a variety of funny, bizarre, and truly stupid quotes.

The same can also be said about managers with some of the most hilarious sound bites coming from the dug out – and none more so than former Spurs boss Harry Redknapp.

He is much-loved for not only taking the north Londoners to the Champions League for the first time in their history, but for also providing a constant stream of entertaining remarks.

Whether it's a post-match outburst at a referee, a sarcastic take on a player's performance or a jibe at the modern-day footballer, Redknapp always delivers a brilliant one-liner.

Fellow managers Glenn Hoddle, Martin Jol and Tim Sherwood have come out with some classic statements, while ex-chairman Alan Sugar was never afraid to speak his mind.

Words of wisdom from the likes of Dele Alli, Les Ferdinand, Danny Blanchflower and the outspoken Benoit Assou-Ekotto have also been hugely amusing.

Many of their funniest comments and loads more can be found in this rib-tickling collection of Spurs quotations. Enjoy!

**Gordon Law**

# THE FUNNIEST SPURS QUOTES... EVER!

# PLAYER POWER

"When a player had the ball and didn't know what to do with it, he'd say, 'The birds are flapping in your head'."

**Ledley King on manager Martin Jol talking double Dutch**

"A man capable of breaking both leg and wind at the same time."

**Jimmy Greaves on Paul Gascoigne**

"Do I wanna go Hull City? NO. Do I wanna go Stoke? NO. Do I wanna go Sunderland? Yes."

**Darren Bent manages to arrange a transfer through Twitter**

**Sebastien Bassong:** "Come on Ade, you earn £200,000-a-week, and you haven't paid £50 to the charity for being the worst player last week."

**Emmanuel Adebayor:** "Don't insult me... I earn 225 [thousand pounds a week]."

"There was certainly discontent in the dressing room. Everyone knows about his man management skills – or lack of them."

**Neil Sullivan is not a fan of Glenn Hoddle**

"I don't call footballers in my team. I don't believe in friendships in football."

**Benoit Assou-Ekotto doesn't want friends**

"Harry [Redknapp] is very similar to [Slaven] Bilic, but is scarier in the dressing room if we're losing at half-time."

**Luka Modric longs for a half-time lead**

"I may have been dirty sometimes, but I never got sent off in my whole life, even as a schoolboy."

**Hard man Dave Mackay**

"I must say that I have seen quite a few Spurs players kiss the badge and then f*ck off. I am still here."

**Benoit Assou-Ekotto is ever loyal**

"He said about four words to me in two years. With Juande [Ramos] and the Spanish [coaches] it was a bit hard. When the manager isn't talking to you it's hard and you start to question their motives."

**Darren Bent gets paranoid**

"It would be great to have him in my [Brazil] team, but he was born in Wales."

**Sandro momentarily forgets Gareth Bale plays for a different country**

"Jermain [Defoe] is only five foot but he was about eight foot before the game."

**Robbie Keane looks up to his teammate**

"I don't know what he looks like. I don't know him, I don't follow this kind of news."

**Benoit Assou-Ekotto admits he has no idea who Spurs' new signing Paulinho is**

"It's like two or three years ago, Rafael van der Vaart was there in training one day. I said 'hello' to him but I didn't know he was Rafael van der Vaart."

**It seems to be a recurring theme for Benoit Assou-Ekotto**

"I've almost got a beard."

**Vedran Corluka on his vow to not shave while Spurs remain unbeaten**

"Well Tim, I guess my advice to you would be this: make as many saves as you can."

**Kasey Keller gives some words of wisdom to fellow countryman Tim Howard after he signed for Manchester United**

"Microsoft bought Skype for 8.5 billion dollars. LOL idiots. They could have downloaded it for free!"

**Dele Alli tweets**

"My mum's run off with the match ball for safe-keeping!"

**Darren Bent wants his ball back after scoring a hat-trick against Dinamo Zagreb**

THE FUNNIEST SPURS QUOTES... EVER!

"Younes would not join Sunderland – even if there was an earthquake."

**Younes Kaboul's agent Rudy Raba in 2008. The defender actually ended up there in 2015 – despite any natural disasters**

"Look, Darth Vader could come to Spurs. I don't care. If he does his job well I am happy for Spurs."

**Benoit Assou-Ekotto Feels the Force**

"For Christmas, I'd get Ben Davis some tissues for after when England beat Wales in the Euros."

**Dele Alli's banter with his Welsh teammate**

**Hazel O'Sullivan:** "When did you get fined for not showing up to training? Just saw on Twitter."

**Andros Townsend:** "Huh? I got fined? Show me."

Hazel posts a screen grab from the Football Manager game.

**Hazel:** "Maybe it's a joke isn't it?"

**Andros:** "Hahahahaha are you joking??"

**Hazel:** "I dunno?"

**Andros Townsend's girlfriend Hazel thought the winger had been fined after seeing a Football Manager screen grab on Twitter**

"Bloody foreigner."

**Ossie Ardiles is upset by diving from Middlesbrough's Bosko Jankovic**

# THE FUNNIEST SPURS QUOTES... EVER!

# CAN YOU MANAGE?

## THE FUNNIEST SPURS QUOTES... EVER!

"I should get out now – I've taken this team as far as I can."

**Harry Redknapp after guiding new club Spurs to five wins out of six**

"I'm like a maestro from the Boston Philarmonic whose biggest breakthrough as a leader was realising that he didn't make any sound himself; the players did."

**Andre Villas-Boas' profound words shortly before being sacked**

"We like a tackle at Tottenham. We're not pansies, you know."

**David Pleat is no southern softy**

"Really I'd want to win everything, whether it's a cup competition or the Premier League or the UEFA Cup."

**Juande Ramos doesn't quite get the cup format of the UEFA Cup**

"I've not done well in this game because I'm a mug."

**Harry Redknapp after guiding Spurs into the Champions League in 2010**

"There's no better feeling in the world than to win in the last minute, though your wife might disagree."

**Martin Jol gets fruity**

"As a manager, you are always under pressure. It always depends on the sack. For me to be here, or not to be – that is the question."
**Mauricio Pochettino uses Shakespeare to play down links with Man United**

"We're down to the bare bones."
**Harry Redknapp's familiar phrase, citing injury problems in his squad, when looking to acquire new players**

"It's like a child, sometimes you have to give them a sweet, when they are bad you have to shout at them."
**Juande Ramos feels like a parent**

"Two [substitutes] were asleep with hats pulled down and blankets over them. I said, 'I'm sorry to drag you up here, I know it's cold and you could be home with the missus with a cup of tea. It's hard for 30 grand a week to watch the game."

**Harry Redknapp's sarcastic take on the modern-day substitute**

"If you have a supply teacher who comes into your school, sometimes they're not treated with the respect that a headmaster is."

**Manager Tim Sherwood on being viewed by the Tottenham players**

"I don't look at my contracts, I don't read one word, I sign at the bottom. Then my accountant rings up and says, 'Harry you've got a £500,000 bonus from the Champions League'."

**Harry Redknapp on picking up bonuses**

"Intelligence doesn't make you a good footballer. Oxford and Cambridge would have the best sides if that were true. It's a football brain that matters and that doesn't usually go with an academic brain. I prefer players not to be too good or too clever at other things. It means they concentrate on football."

**Bill Nicholson wants players to have their brains in their feet**

# Can You Manage?

"Hello, my name is Jacques. I am 53 years old and I live in London."

**Jacques Santini greets the Spurs players in bizarre fashion on his first day in 2004**

"I am completely and utterly disorganised. I write like a two-year-old and I can't spell. I can't work a computer, I don't know what an email is, I have never sent a fax and I've never even sent a text message."

**Harry Redknapp the technophobe**

"I don't think I'm the big bad wolf. I can't produce the money to buy players."

**David Pleat defends his transfer record**

"If you pay them the wages they'll come. We all kid ourselves: 'I've wanted to play for Tottenham since I was two, I had pictures of Jimmy Greaves on my wall'. It's a load of bull. Here's £80,000 a week. Lovely jubbly."

**Harry Redknapp on overseas players**

"I didn't want to talk to people for three weeks after the defeat. I touched my wife but didn't speak to her."

**Martin Jol after losing to West Ham**

"We've won seven out the last eight league games, and we can't do any more than that."

**Harry Redknapp. Maybe win eight?**

## Can You Manage?

"It reminds me of my first date with my girlfriend Karina, who is now my wife, when I was a player. She said to me, 'Let's go to see a movie at the cinema after the game' and it was a Shakespeare film. I was very tired after the game and I thought, 'Shakespeare? For me?' It was very boring. Then, suddenly, I felt an elbow in my ribs and I sat up quickly, wondering what was happening... and I had been snoring. Do I want to sign a new contract? Yes, why not?"

**Mauricio Pochettino uses another Shakespeare analogy when talking about being offered a new Spurs deal**

"All that stuff about the Spurs tradition for attractive football is just a crutch. They haven't been playing like that for ages."

**George Graham shortly after becoming manager in 1998**

"I'm not a wheeler dealer, f*ck off. I'm not a f*cking wheeler and dealer, don't even, don't say that, I'm a f*cking football manager."

**Harry Redknapp on his transfer reputation**

"I've introduced something new to the training. It's called running."

**Gerry Francis after being appointed Spurs boss in 1994**

# Can You Manage?

"It's like when you are in love with some lady. There are a lot of women around the world, but you want only one. Sometimes it is impossible. It's about love. And in football it is the same."
**Mauricio Pochettino compares Tottenham's chasing of West Brom striker Saido Berahino with a frustrated love affair**

"You can never compare two players that are different, they're never going to be the same."
**Glenn Hoddle. OK then...**

"I haven't seen my missus, Sandra, all week. She might be delighted, I am not."
**Harry Redknapp is a workaholic**

"I think it's like what Britney Spears and Will.I.Am sing: 'Everybody in the club, all eyes on us, all eyes on us'. Because it's not important what Arsenal do."

**Mauricio Pochettino, when asked about Arsenal winning the title, he responded by reciting some pop lyrics**

"This is a football club that has been put together by I don't know who, and I don't know how. It's a mishmash of players with people playing where they want to play. It's scary."

**Harry Redknapp on the Tottenham squad he inherited**

"I've found myself on some days leaving home at three in the morning. I'm outside the training ground at five but they don't open up until seven. I'm just sitting there, listening to the radio."

**Harry Redknapp is an insomniac**

"If it was down to me I'd get a 10-year contract now!"

**Tim Sherwood when asked if he wanted the Tottenham job – and he ended up with 18 months**

"When I was aged 12 or 13, boys would meet their football manager dressed in a blazer or at least a pair of trousers. Now some of them turn up to see me, wearing a pair of jeans with their a*se hanging out. They just don't care."

**Harry Redknapp on kids today**

"Defoe was nibbling his arm, but if you ask Mascherano to show you any marks on it he will not be able to. Mascherano had kicked Jermain from behind three times and Defoe wanted to show his frustration in a nice, comical way."

**Martin Jol plays down claims that Jermain Defoe took a bite out of West Ham's Javier Mascherano**

# Can You Manage?

"If you lose a few games, some people call these silly phone-ins and say, 'They were rubbish today, they were absolutely useless' when they weren't even at the game. They were listening to it on the radio or out shopping with the wife. I don't listen to them. I turn the radio on and put Magic FM on instead. I don't want to listen to a bunch of idiots. They must have sad lives."

**Harry Redknapp fumes at phone-ins**

"A big club will always go for a big name, a sexy name. You'll have to ask my wife if I'm sexy – she'll definitely say no!"

**Harry Redknapp being modest**

# REFFING HELL

"Nani put his hands on the ball. It was deliberate handball and the assistant referee sees it. It was a free-kick to us but I don't think the referee saw it. I think Mark Clattenburg is a good ref but he made a mess of this. It was a scandalous decision and a farcical way to end the game. But the officials will come up with a story that will make it look right."

**Harry Redknapp blasts referee Mark Clattenburg after Man United's Nani controversially scored into an empty net, while Spurs keeper Heurelho Gomes was preparing to take what he believed was a free-kick**

"If they want to make an issue of what I said then I'll make some issues as well, don't worry. Don't expect me to come out on the TV any-more – ever – and speak to the press after a game. Otherwise, what chance have we got? If you want me just to come and talk rubbish and say, 'No, it was a good decision, I'm quite hap-py with it', then don't bother to get me to come out after a game... I don't want to go on TV; I'd much rather stay in the dressing room with the players. But when I'm asked a question, I give a truthful answer. He [Clattenburg] made a right mess of it all, and that was my answer. And I stand by that 100 per cent."

**Redknapp says he won't speak to the media if the FA charge him for criticising Clattenburg over Nani's freak goal**

"Yes, I swear a lot. But the advantage is that having played abroad I can choose a different language from the referee's."
**Jurgen Klinsmann**

"I never walk in after games and complain about a referee but this guy is scary. He's a poor referee and I've seen him make a mess of so many games. He's really not good enough."
**Harry Redknapp on 'scary' Steve Tanner's display in a 2-0 defeat at West Brom**

"The penalty – I have to choose my words very carefully – it was a disgrace."
**Robbie Keane changes his tune mid-sentence**

"It was a penalty, a blatant penalty. How he [Webb] can book him... I've never been one for criticising referees – it's never been my game – but it was a blatant penalty. If you get the penalty, it could make a big difference."

**Harry Redknapp criticises referee Howard Webb for turning down a penalty claim and for not sending off Sunderland's Lee Cattermole**

"It was Mary Decker and Zola Budd."

**Harry Redknapp sympathises with Rafael's red card for Man United at White Hart Lane, referring to the athletes' infamous coming together at the 1984 Olympic Games**

"That's why we've come away with nothing, two decisions have been completely and utterly wrong. I spoke to the referee after the game. I never go and speak to referees after the game, I accept defeat and have never complained about refereeing decisions in 30 years of managing. Never. But today he got some badly wrong. When he goes home tonight and sees them he'll know he's made a couple of terrible decisions. The linesman, he'll watch it tonight, when his wife's making him a bacon sandwich and he'll think: 'F*ck me what have I done there today?"

**Harry Redknapp blasts Chris Foy for failing to spot Ryan Shawcross' hand ball which stopped Younes Kaboul's goal-bound effort**

"It's always better to have two goalkeepers than one, but I'm always prepared to accept the referee's decision."
**Danny Blanchflower on a potential hand ball by Peter Baker at Fulham**

"I've had so many cards it feels like Christmas."
**Edgar Davids on his stream of yellows**

"If he is cuddling him then I would be a bit frustrated that's for sure."
**Martin Jol on managers getting friendly with referees**

# THE FUNNIEST SPURS QUOTES... EVER!

# LIFESTYLE CHOICE

"The spirit he has shown has been second to none."

**Terry Venables' unfortunate choice of words after Terry Fenwick's drink-driving charge**

"You could buy 10 penthouses up north for the price of something down here, house prices are a joke! They are. It's unbelievable."

**Jonathan Woodgate**

"I don't go out, so I don't get attention from girls. They're not going to have posters of me on their walls."

**Gareth Bale**

# Lifestyle Choice

"I know the odd indulgence doesn't hurt
players from time to time... besides, what
can you do? Can you follow a player home
to check if his missus is giving him steak and
kidney pie for tea instead of pasta?"

**Harry Redknapp**

"I know women are stronger than we are. But I
play football, I make the money."

**David Ginola**

"I am here to earn big money at Tottenham and
to meet English girls."

**Moussa Saib on his arrival at Spurs**

"I'll implement a strong rule next season that drinking is a no-no here. Footballers should dedicate their lives to playing. Footballers should not drink. You shouldn't put diesel in a Ferrari. I know it's hard but they are earning big money, they are role models to kids."

**Harry Redknapp after Ledley King was arrested outside a London nightclub**

"Our defenders, [Gary] Doherty and Anthony Gardner, were fantastic and I told them that when they go to bed tonight, they should think of each other."

**David Pleat**

"Coping with the language shouldn't prove a problem. I can't even speak English yet."
**Paul Gascoigne after agreeing to join Lazio**

**Q:** "Who is the person you'd least like to be stuck in a lift with?"
**A:** "Glenn Hoddle, if he was singing."
**Les Ferdinand**

"If you can't pass the ball properly, a bowl of pasta's not going to make that much difference!"
**Harry Redknapp, when asked if a change of diet had contributed to Tottenham's 4-4 draw at Arsenal**

"I don't think he's a boy to go abroad. The first chance he gets, he goes back to his family in Wales."

**Harry Redknapp on Gareth Bale in 2012. Months later, he joins Real Madrid**

"The biggest problem in England is driving on the left side – but I haven't hit anyone yet."

**Rafael van der Vaart**

"I'd look out of my bedroom window and see friends of mine kissing some girl. I'd say, 'Can't I go out for half an hour?' My mum said, 'One day you will thank me'. I thank her every day."

**Jermain Defoe on his mum Sandra**

"Gary Mabbutt, Teddy Sheringham, Colin Calderwood, I had a whole group of guys who showed me 'this is how things work here'. Fish and chips. We go down the street, to a cafe and we figure it out. This is how it works in London, the rivalries, the Premier League, life off the field."

**Jurgen Klinsmann on players' diets**

"I promised Daniel last night to sing together if we win a title."

**Mauricio Pochettino promises to get the mic out with chairman Daniel Levy**

"When I am at work, I do my job 100 per cent. But after, I am like a tourist in London. I have my Oyster card and I take the Tube. I eat."
**Benoit Assou-Ekotto says football is just a job to him**

"I still don't like calling her a dog, she was so much better than that."
**Harry Redknapp on his dog Rosie**

"Nandos isn't a nandos without fanta and coke mixed #fantoke"
**Dele Alli tweets about his unique soft drink combination**

"What a nightmare. I'm a Tottenham fan and I get cuffed to you."

**A fellow prisoner to Tony Adams after the Arsenal defender's arrest for drink-driving**

"We've got sports scientists who insist it's important for the lads to eat after games to refuel, even if it's 2am. I used to refuel after games at West Ham until half past three in the morning in a different way – but then I'm old school."

**Harry Redknapp**

"I'm no poof that's for sure."

**Paul Gascoigne on Terry Wogan's show in 1990**

"I always ended up losing because I would get the ball to me and not pass to the others. I couldn't understand why I was losing, but I can't dribble on the FIFA game."

**Christian Eriksen, with a dribbling rating of 83, is frustrated playing himself on FIFA 16**

"Do you think Paolo Maldini at 41 is going out on a Saturday night and drinking with lager coming out of his ears and falling over? I don't see it somehow."

**Harry Redknapp on English football's love of a pint**

"Ossie [Ardiles] came in the dressing room after the game and handed us £20 or £30 each. He just said: 'Have a good time.' So we all went to the pub. That was wonderful, the simplicity of getting together, getting us working as hard as we could and enjoying the company of everyone."

**Jurgen Klinsmann**

"I'm devastated to be honest. That was probably the biggest blow of the year for me when they got voted out. For me, they should have won and gone all the way. They were the most entertaining."

**Peter Crouch is gutted Jedward were voted out of The X Factor**

"That's part of the territory. I wouldn't go out and get drunk and start falling around or pulling some old slag tomorrow night, would I? I'm not that stupid. Because somebody will catch you out. Having said that, Tiger Woods didn't do too bad."

**Harry Redknapp**

"On Tuesday nights you don't want to be at home watching EastEnders, you want to be at the Lane and playing against the great players of the world."

**Jermain Defoe would rather avoid the soaps**

**Lifestyle Choice**

"I've had a bed made which is very nice. It's obviously a bit longer so my feet don't stick out the bed now. But I actually prefer them sticking out as I got used to it, so I still hang them off the side."

**Peter Crouch on life as a very tall person**

"Once we had a players' karaoke party. Gazza took off his clothes and sang Rod Stewart's 'Do You Think I'm Sexy?' There is no one like him. I wish we had someone like him. We Norwegians are boring."

**Erik Thorstvedt on Paul Gascoigne's social habits**

"Sometimes it's got to the stage now where I hate Saturday nights, because jack sh*t knows what's coming in the papers on Sunday. I tell you what was the worst one, the Gaza Strip. You know the term the Gaza Strip, remember that? That was murder for me. I'd be sitting there having a shave and that, and the news would come on, 'And the Gazza...', and I'd be like, 'What's that?!', and I realised it was the Gaza Strip. I couldn't wait for that to end."

**Paul Gascoigne says he used to get paranoid when Gaza was mentioned on news programmes**

"I got some sweets and the next thing I felt someone pull my overcoat. There are two guys on their knees in front of me and they've got my trousers and they keep pulling them. I'm pushing them away but while I'm doing that they're rifling my pockets."

**Harry Redknapp has his sweets stolen in Madrid**

"Jermaine is really generous – he bought me some Christian Louboutin shoes for Christmas which I love. But the best present he ever got is priceless – a tattoo of my face on his forearm."

**Jermaine Jenas' fiancee Ellie**

# THE FUNNIEST SPURS QUOTES... EVER!

# BEST OF ENEMIES

"If Osvaldo Ardiles had gone to Arsenal, they'd have had him marking the opposing keeper."

**Danny Blanchflower has a pop at the rivals**

"There's no problem with Jermain. I wouldn't swap him for Miss World – he would probably swap me for Miss World though."

**Martin Jol after talk of a bust-up with Jermain Defoe**

"I grew up in a Tottenham-supporting area and most of my mates follow Spurs. They used to give me all sorts of stick when I played for Arsenal."

**David Bentley on the rivalry with Arsenal**

"Because of his pride, Hoddle wanted to be the best player in training every day – at 46 years of age. I don't think you can see the whole picture when you're training out there among the guys. Can you imagine Arsene Wenger playing with Thierry Henry and the rest?"

**David Pleat on Glenn Hoddle's demise as manager**

"He's a coward who will not stand up and admit mistakes. I got mugged into believing that this Adonis of the football world was the be-all and end-all in management skill and tactics. In my time at Tottenham I made lots of mistakes. The biggest was possibly employing him."

**Alan Sugar on George Graham**

"When you are a person of a certain age, with a certain intelligence like he is, then why if you are the manager, would you be jealous of someone who is playing well and is loved by the fans."

**David Ginola on George Graham**

"[George] Graham would always give me hassle. I knew he wasn't a big fan of mine, but he should have respected what I could do. He would try to put me down in front of other players. Even if I had been the best on the pitch he would point to me and say, 'I expect more from you'. He never did that to anyone else."

**Ginola wasn't loved by manager Graham**

"The trouble with Christian Gross is that no one had heard of him. The communication was not brilliant and I decided, as captain, to explain to him how things worked and what players liked and were used to. I do not believe he listened to a word I said."

**Gary Mabbutt's words fall on deaf ears**

"No one at Tottenham would shed a single tear if Glenn Hoddle was sacked tomorrow. The only way they will bring success back to Tottenham is through a change of manager."

**Tim Sherwood**

"When you finish playing football, young man, which is going to be very soon, I feel, you'll make a very good security guard."
**David Pleat to 17-year-old Neil Ruddock**

"At least all the aggravation will keep me slim."
**George Graham on taking flak from Spurs fans for his Arsenal history**

"The Germans were better than us. Then, at 4-1, we needed a goal and we took off [Jermain] Defoe and sent on [Emile] Heskey!"
**Harry Redknapp attacks England manager Fabio Capello after the defeat to Germany in the 2010 World Cup**

"I did really well to hold myself back. I really don't think he realises how strong I am, otherwise he wouldn't approach me with headbutts and everything."

**Martin Jol after a touchline spat with Arsene Wenger in April 2006**

"I do hate Arsenal. With a passion. No money in the word would ever tempt me to play for them."

**Spurs fan Teddy Sheringham**

"Arsenal winning the Champions League would be a nightmare."

**Martin Jol**

"When I say that he needs to stand up and be counted, I mean that he needs to sit down and take a look at himself in the mirror."

**Gary Mabbutt's changing advice to Sir Alex Ferguson**

"If I would have £2bn I would buy Arsenal. And I'd make a big parking place from the Emirates and make a new stadium for Spurs. Or for another club, you know. That is a nice [idea]!"

**Martin Jol**

"What's happening? F*ck all and it's starting to wind me up!! Sort it out Harry for f*ck sake."

**David Bentley's wife Kimberley tweets**

"He says he didn't see me or hear me but he's two bob he is, two bob."

**Coach Clive Allen claims Arsene Wenger refused to shake his hand after the derby**

"It goes in one ear and comes out the other."

**Andre-Villas Boas on France coach Didier Deschamps' complaints that Hugo Lloris' is second choice at Spurs. Deschamps replied: "I have two ears as well. What he says has the same effect on me."**

"I definitely wouldn't play for Arsenal, that's for sure."

**Darren Anderton**

"Did I feel Lens didn't do its best to keep me? Of course. If they cannot manage a strong character, they prefer to part with him. At Lens, they love sheep, but I am not one."

**Benoit Assou-Ekotto attacks old club Lens**

"I don't want to know who is my enemy. All I want to know is who are my friends. My friends are Tottenham fans today. I play for Tottenham. I don't care about Arsenal."

**The ever-popular Emmanuel Adebayor**

"If Bergkamp thinks he's gonna set the world alight he can forget it. When the fog, ice and cold arrive, he won't want to know."

**Alan Sugar. Well, he got that one wrong**

"It's been a long time since Glenn Hoddle's managed a football team and the game has moved on significantly."

**Manager Tim Sherwood replies to Glenn Hoddle's claim that Spurs are lacking in motivation**

"Kevin Keegan has approached me and they've offered me more money. I am definitely leaving Spurs. It's all about the money. I don't care about the [League Cup] final, I don't care about the cup."

**Pascal Chimbonda shows his, ahem, loyalty to Tottenham**

"If you dress poorly, he mocks you for days! Then he'll buy you a drink, and you'll think he's now your best friend. But if you make a mistake, he'll kill you!"

**Emmanuel Adebayor on Jose Mourinho**

"In order to get the success the fans crave, in my opinion, there is only one solution. Give David [Pleat] the job because the position he holds at the club is making it enormously difficult for a manager to succeed. He was so obstructive towards me, never working in harmony with me and always working towards his own end."

**Glenn Hoddle on Tottenham's director of football David Pleat**

"Even if Tottenham were on top of the league, I would not regret my transfer... If you lose there [in England], nobody supports you in the stadium."

**Nabil Bentaleb criticises Tottenham and their 'fickle' fans after joining Schalke on loan**

"Just saw Barthez comments. I normally don't comment on such crap but when disrespected by someone I don't respect I must. Barthez was ignorant, disrespectful and out of order to mention my name."

**Brad Friedel fires a shot at Fabien Barthez who said Hugo Lloris should have his place in the team**

# THE FUNNIEST SPURS QUOTES... EVER!

# CALL THE MANAGER

"I'm feeling like a drunk who hasn't got a drink. I'd never heard of Groundhog Day until recently but now I must go and see the film."
**David Pleat after Spurs throw away another lead to draw 4-4 against Leicester**

"I have to laugh when I see Harry [Redknapp] spending millions at Tottenham. When I was manager there, I had to lend THEM money."
**Gerry Francis**

"They can offer him free chicken for life and we can't compete with that."
**Harry Redknapp says Blackburn have a better chance of signing David Beckham**

"As England manager you know that you're probably the most hated man in the county, apart from the Chancellor [of the Exchequer].

**Spurs boss Ossie Ardiles rules himself out of the England job**

"To be fair, when you looked at our run-in, it was almost scary."

**Manager Harry Redknapp on Tottenham's 'frightening' fixture list at the end of 2009/10**

"I was nervous towards the end. My heart rate was 189. Almost a heart attack."

**Martin Jol after Tottenham's win over Chelsea in 2006**

"The day I got married, Teddy Sheringham asked for a transfer. I spent my honeymoon in a hotel room with a fax machine trying to sign a replacement."
**Gerry Francis**

"If you asked me if I wanted to sell my car and I said 'no', that is the end of it. You don't keep ringing me up."
**Harry Redknapp hits out at Sunderland for their never-ending pursuit of Darren Bent**

"I've changed. It's all attack now... only kidding."
**George Graham after a 5-2 win over Watford in 1999**

"I thought Nasri might be captain for them, so they would have to shake hands, then we could get them in a room before the game and William could bash him up or something."
**Harry Redknapp after making William Gallas skipper against Arsenal. Samir Nasri refused to shake the hand of Gallas because of previous bad blood**

"The man we want has to fit a certain profile. Is he a top coach? Would the players respect him? Is he a nutcase?"
**David Pleat, director of football, on finding Glenn Hoddle's replacement**

"I have had a drink with them in the dressing room – even though you cannot tell. It's quite a nice diet and sometimes it lets them eat and drink totally out of control – and yes, that includes champagne."

**Juande Ramos after the League Cup final victory over Chelsea**

"I got the right hump with Gareth [Bale] when their right-back [Bacary Sagna] made a diabolical tackle on him and then Gareth went for a tackle and bumped in and then walked over and shook hands with him. I said, 'What are we? Are we the nice guys or something?'"

**Harry Redknapp on Spurs' comeback to win 3-2 against Arsenal**

"[Gennaro] Gattuso had a flare-up with Joe Jordan. I don't know why. He obviously hadn't done his homework. He could've picked a fight with somebody else. I know who I'd pick between Joe Jordan and Gennaro Gattuso anyway... Joe all night long. All night long. He's lucky Joe didn't take his teeth out!"

**Harry Redknapp backs his coach as the game against Milan got heated**

"They have treatment three times a day, once in the morning, once at lunchtime and again at 4pm, which gets them out of here just in time for rush hour on the M25. It's amazing how quickly they're all improving."

**George Graham**

"I read in the papers that Terry Neill says he's going to put the joy back in Spurs' football. What's he going to do – give them bloody banjos?"

**Eddie Baily, the former assistant manager of Bill Nicholson, in 1974**

"I remember meeting Vinny Samways for the first time at a Bobby Charlton coaching school I did about 30 years ago. He was nine at the time, and I remember after that, dropping him home a few times because his dad was doing 25 years for armed robbery!"

**Harry Redknapp**

"Too many of them are too nice to each other. We need to show a bit more guts and not want to be someone's mate all the time. There's a few I'd count on. There's a few I wouldn't. I'm not going to forget about this by the time we get on the motorway."

**Tim Sherwood after a 4-0 defeat by Chelsea**


"We are moving on, you can't dwell on it. They are all men, they all appreciate that I am singing it from the heart, not from the script – I'm not an actor, I work on impulse. I'm never going to take a step back. I'm just going to shoot from the hip. That's what I'm like. I'm a manager, not a babysitter."

**Sherwood reflects a few days later**

"I'll just have a bacon sandwich, a cup of tea and take my dogs out. I've had ups and downs, life is a roller coaster and I try not to get too down or go overboard. It was always going to be nervy. If people thought we were going to smash Milan out of sight, they've not been watching football. We were playing AC Milan, who are top of Serie A and have lost only three games all season, not Raggy-Arsed Rovers."
**Harry Redknapp reflects on Spurs reaching the Champions League quarter-finals**

"We tried everything to get him. Maybe they offered Sharon Stone."
**Ossie Ardiles on missing out on Philippe Albert, who joined Newcastle United**

"I thought his team were very good and showed a lot of class. It's just a shame... [their manager did not]. In the first two minutes, he was going over to the fourth official saying I was stepping in his box. Waving goodbye like that? It lacks class. Why would anyone do that? He's got a good side, of course he has, but not for me thank you. I have no intention of speaking to him."

**Tim Sherwood on a touchline row with Benfica manager Jorge Jesus**

"I thought I was David Pleat as I was running up the touchline to celebrate – except I haven't got his colour shoes."

**Harry Redknapp on recreating the Pleat jig**

# THE FUNNIEST SPURS QUOTES... EVER!

# A FUNNY
# OLD GAME

"The atmosphere in the dressing room has changed completely. We feel more at ease. It is because Harry Redknapp is a very colourful person – we joke that he looks as if he comes to the stadium straight from the pub."
**Roman Pavlyuchenko on his manager. Redknapp replied: "Maybe he's not used to seeing a manager with a smile on his face, but I haven't been to a pub for about 30 years – honest!"**

**Duchess of Kent [at the 1961 FA Cup Final]:** "Why do the other team have their names on their tracksuits and yours don't?"
**Danny Blanchflower:** "Ah well, ma'am, you see we all know each other."

"It was like asking Frank Sinatra to sing in front of three-dozen people."

**Spurs striker Jimmy Greaves describes playing in front of small crowds for England at the 1962 World Cup**

"Being a Spurs fan as a boy and a player for so many years, it would be hard to sign for Arsenal. I don't think the fans here would ever forgive me."

**Sol Campbell not long before he did!**

"No one wants to commit hari-kari and sell themselves down the river."

**Gary Lineker on England duty at Euro 92**

"Eccentric, yes of course you can be, absolutely. But to be a top goalkeeper you can't be thick."
**Brad Freidel**

"I'm 58 and I think even I've played more football than [Darren] Anderton over the past two years. If the Black Death ever swept through London again, I would not even want to be in the next street to him because you can be sure he would get it."
**Jimmy Greaves on the man called 'Sicknote'**

"If we don't know what we're going to do, how can the other side?"
**Danny Blanchflower**

"I was on £13,500 per week... I had muppets as teammates who were on treble the money."
**Sol Campbell on his old Spurs colleagues**

**Interviewer:** "Well Danny, what is the secret to the Spurs winning every match so far this season?"
**Danny Blanchflower:** "Most probably because in each match we have scored more goals than our opponents."

"Me, dive? Never. I always go straight for goal."
**Jurgen Klinsmann**

"There are days when you think about it more than others and I even find myself talking to my leg, saying, 'Please don't let me down again'."
**Jamie Redknapp conversing with his knee**

"There has been speculation about me being wanted by Spurs and talk of me going back to London. But all that talk about the bright lights of the capital is cr*p."
**Tim Sherwood, of Blackburn Rovers, shortly before signing for Tottenham**

"Darren Anderton has had so many X-rays that he got radiation sickness."
**Alan Sugar**

# A Funny Old Game

"Jimmy Greaves would walk past four defenders, send the goalie one way, roll the ball into the opposite corner and walk away as if to say, 'What am I here for?' Then have a fag at half-time."

**Harry Redknapp on the legendary Spurs striker**

"The whole problem with football players is they really take themselves seriously. We kick a ball around and we earn 100,000, 200,000 or even 300,000 euros a week. We don't improve the world. It's not like we invented hot water."

**Benoit Assou-Ekoto keeps it real**

"I've not seen it. I'll have to see it on TV."

**Michael Dawson's verdict on his own possible hand ball which led to Spurs' equaliser at Aston Villa**

"I feel like Superman. I could fly home."

**David Bentley after his wonder goal in a 4-4 draw against his old side Arsenal**

**A young Nobby Stiles:** "Blanchflower, you're finished!"

**Danny Blanchflower:** "Excuse me son, I haven't read the programme yet. What's your name?"

"I heard Simon Davies shout, 'Les, look out, there's a bottle coming' and luckily it didn't hit me. But it must have been close because I could smell the beer that came out of it as it passed me."

**Les Ferdinand on crowd trouble during a League Cup tie at Chelsea**

"We signed @VictorWanyama and he was very nice we enjoyed it."

**Tottenham's Twitter account has a laugh, referring to Victor Wanyama's classic "I had spaghetti and it was very nice I enjoyed it" tweet in 2012**

"Whenever I break down with injury, it's always 'Sicknote'. People read it and think it's funny. I've been out on the street, just walking along, and they shout, 'Sicknote!' It's not nice."
**Darren Anderton**

"As we went out on the pitch, he handed me a piece of paper. It was the evening menu for the Liverpool Royal Infirmary."
**Jimmy Greaves on Liverpool hard man Tommy Smith**

"I don't have any particular celebration – a big smile is all you need."
**Dimitar Berbatov keeps it simple**

"I had never heard of Sheriff Tiraspol before – I thought they were from Northern Ireland! I only found out 20 minutes before we landed. I got told it was a country within Moldova. That was a new one for me, but it has improved my geography! I am very pleased to be here. I can tell my grandchildren that I played in a part of Moldova that isn't Moldova."

**Lewis Holtby on Tottenham's Europa League trip to Tiraspol**

"In Africa, when I was younger, what was I playing for? I remember playing for bananas. I remember playing for water. I don't play for a contract. I love the game."

**Emmanuel Adebayor**

"I looked at my watch and saw that the training session had gone on for exactly two hours! Then another half an hour in the gym! Two-and-a-half hours! Can you imagine that? I trained like never in my life before, I swear! The weights started to get to me and I stopped and said to the trainer, 'I can't do this'. That's how they work – I'm shocked. I thought it would be a lot easier."

**Roman Pavlyuchenko is surprised at Spurs' training methods**

"Oh I'm sorry – I don't follow football."

**William Gallas after talking up Milan's Antonio Cassano and then told he was ineligible to play in the Champions League**

"I just didn't know what to do. I ran one way, then another, looking for my dad. All of a sudden they were kicking off. I'd like to think it will be up there when it comes to goal of the season. I hope my mum taped it."

**Danny Rose after scoring a 30-yard volley on his debut against Arsenal**

"Brutal but very funny. The biggest capitulation since Newcastle in the 90s."

**Tottenham Hotspur's tweet poking fun at Liverpool's 2014 title collapse. It was later deleted after Spurs claimed their Vine account was "compromised"**

# THE FUNNIEST SPURS QUOTES... EVER!

# MEDIA CIRCUS

**Journalist:** "What do you feel you have added to Spurs?"

**George Graham:** "Me."

"I don't want them going out having Christmas parties. What chance have you got? The press will be waiting, someone will be taking pictures of them. Somebody can just have their eyes closed and it looks like they are boozed. You don't need it."

**Harry Redknapp**

"Football journalists? They're just about able to do joined-up writing."

**Sir Alan Sugar**

"I want this to become my ticket to the dreams!"
**Christian Gross shouts in broken English
to the press on his first day, while waving a
Travelcard**

"Maybe I can ask you the first question. Are
there any diving schools in London?"
**Jurgen Klinsmann to the press on joining
Spurs**

"You weren't allowed to speak to the press
when I was playing. If you got caught, you got a
fine of a week's wages, which was about £7."
**Harry Redknapp**

"You're going to write what you want to write and to f*ck me up on cup final day – I know what's going to happen Rob and you're all barking up the wrong tree. If you say the tax hasn't been declared and it hasn't been paid, I will sue the b*llocks off, yeah everybody at the News of the World, make no mistake, yeah."

**Harry Redknapp to News of the World reporter Rob Beasley ahead of the 2009 League Cup final against Man United**

**Journalist:** "Is [Jurgen] Klinsmann Spurs' biggest-ever signing?"

**Ossie Ardiles:** "No, I was."

**Andre Villas-Boas gets a bit narky with a reporter when asked about keeper Hugo Lloris' "frustration" at being left out of the Spurs side.**

**Villas-Boas:** "What is the frustration?"

**Journalist:** "Well, the frustration at not being in the team."

**Villas-Boas:** "How do you know?"

**Journalist:** "Well, he didn't play last night, did he?"

**Villas-Boas:** "How do you know he's frustrated?"

**Journalist:** "No, I'm asking you, do you find him frustrated?"

**Ouch!**

# TALKING BALLS

"We're moving up the table now which is hopefully the right direction."

**Paul Robinson is getting the idea of football after Tottenham's win over Portsmouth**

"Adele might set fire to the rain... But SpongeBob can make a campfire under water."

**Dele Alli tweets**

"We don't talk about going higher than fifth, we just want to play well. Then with a bit of luck we can go higher than fifth."

**Kevin-Prince Boateng**

"I cannot tell you what is going to happen tomorrow – only today. And I can not even tell you what is going to happen today."

**David Pleat**

"I expect the Croats to come out... Oh dear, I had better not say fighting, had I?"

**Peter Shreeves before facing Hajduk Split from war-torn Croatia**

"I can't even remember when the Seventies was."

**Robbie Keane**

"It's a no-win game for us, although I suppose we can win by winning."

**Gary Doherty**

"I was disappointed to leave Spurs, but quite pleased that I did."

**Steve Perryman**

"We signed to play until the day we died, and we did."

**Jimmy Greaves**

"I've got a gut feeling in my stomach."

**Alan Sugar**

"We will probably have to score more goals than we let in to win games."

**Jermaine Jenas**

"There is always a place in my heart for Tottingham Hotspurs."

**Ossie Ardiles**

"Everything in our favour was against us."

**Danny Blanchflower**

"What I said to them at half-time would be unprintable on radio."

**Gerry Francis**

"[Ossie] Ardiles always says, 'If you're confident you're always totally different to the player that's lacking confidence'."
**Keith Burkinshaw**

"I was so upset – I felt like my life had been hit by a train."
**Luka Modric after suffering a fractured fibula**

"You can't switch the lights on every time and we didn't smell that one coming. The car was in neutral and we couldn't put it in drive."
**Glenn Hoddle**

"We needed some of these 1-0s, we weren't winning the 1-0s before – we were either drawing or losing."

**Jermaine Jenas on Tottenham's knack of drawing games 1-0**

"This performance today shows that other teams are going to have to score more goals than us if they want to beat us."

**Darren Bent**

"Playing another London side could be an omen, but I don't believe in omens!"

**George Graham**

# THE FUNNIEST SPURS QUOTES... EVER!

"I had mixed feelings – like watching my mother-in-law drive over a cliff in your car."
**Terry Venables**

"I never make predictions and I never will."
**Paul Gascoigne**

"Glenn is putting his head in the frying pan."
**Ossie Ardiles on Glenn Hoddle**

"We all knew we had to roll up our socks."
**Les Ferdinand mixes up his metaphors**

"There's no in between – you're either good or bad. We were in between."
**Gary Lineker**

"I was surprised, but I always say nothing surprises me in football."
**Les Ferdinand**

"All that remains is for a few dots and commas to be crossed."
**Mitchell Thomas**

# THE FUNNIEST SPURS QUOTES... EVER!

# MANAGING PLAYERS

"Not speaking English is a problem. You've always got his interpreter running around the training ground. Sometimes you pass the ball through the middle and he chases it. And the interpreter is running alongside him and he gets in there and heads it into the net."
**Harry Redknapp on Russian striker Roman Pavlyuchenko**

"Palacios is suspended – he likes tackling you see – so I don't know if he'll be any good in our team!"
**Harry Redknapp on new signing Wilson Palacios**

"[Jurgen] Klinsmann has taken to English football like a duck out of water."

**Gerry Francis on the German striker**

"Can you imagine how the players would react if I turned up one day and said, 'I'd like you to meet Cock and Dick'?"

**Martin Jol on why he doesn't have his brothers on the coaching staff. And yes, that is their real names**

"What he can achieve is scary. He has everything – he's six feet, can head it, has a great left foot and great touch."

**Harry Redknapp on 'scary' Gareth Bale**

"How the f*cking hell did he miss that? My missus could have scored that... You keep pussyfooting around with people – what am I supposed to say? Really good try? Really unlucky? He's really done his best with that?"
**Harry Redknapp after Darren Bent misses an easy chance against Portsmouth in 2009**

"Tim Sherwood has come in, done very well and given us another string to the bow in a different type of way."
**Glenn Hoddle**

"He's had a couple of dickie moments..."
**Harry Redknapp on Heurelho Gomes**

"One reason he's improved so much is he's stopped messing about with his barnet."

**Harry Redknapp on Gareth Bale**

"He gets the little sniff type of goals."

**Glenn Hoddle on Steffen Iversen**

"Modric played well. Keane, Defoe and Palacios played well. But I don't want to pick out individuals."

**Harry Redknapp**

"Steven Carr has hit a small blimp."

**Glenn Hoddle**

"I just told [the translator] to tell [Pavlyuchenko] to f*cking run around a bit. The boy himself just kept nodding his head. He might be thinking inside, 'What's this t*sser saying to me?'"
**Harry Redknapp after Roman Pavlyuchenko got the winner against Liverpool in 2008**

"He drove me mad in training. Technically, he was outstanding but he always seemed to be playing with his hair."
**Harry Redknapp on Gareth Bale**

"He is an absolute freak."
**Harry Redknapp on Ledley King's ability to keep playing despite his knee trouble**

"I can swear that it didn't happen. It's the same if you told my wife I'm gay.  A big laugh."

**Martin Jol laughs off talk he was ordered to play Dimitar Berbatov against Chelsea**

"He can't remember too much about what happened. He came over to the bench and said he wanted to carry on, so we told him he was Pele."

**Glenn Hoddle after Les Ferdinand suffered a blow to the head against Everton**

"There's no doubt Bentley has balls – and plenty of 'em."

**Harry Redknapp on David Bentley**

# THE FUNNIEST SPURS QUOTES... EVER!

# BOARDROOM BANTER

"We're 100 per cent behind Terry [Venables] –
I've even taken down my Amstrad satellite dish
and put it in the dustbin."
**Neil Ruddock on the row between manager
Terry Venables and chairman Alan Sugar,
the founder of Amstrad**

"There's a limit to the thickness of the skin of
the rhino. I want a goal at the end of the
rainbow, or at least to be appreciated. What I
won't accept is more abuse. I've been branded
a cold, cynical individual with no knowledge of
football and no interest in the club's heritage or
traditions."
**Alan Sugar on having to deal with fan
protests in 1998**

"We've had everyone. Managers, agents, mothers, fathers, dustmen, cleaners applying."
**David Pleat on finding Glenn Hoddle's replacement in 2003**

"If he put a mask on, then called himself Geraldo Franciso, and came back here tomorrow, things would turn around immediately."
**Alan Sugar after Gerry Francis resigns in 1997**

"If I fail, I'll stand up and be counted – let some other brain surgeon take over."
**Alan Sugar, in 1996**

"[Alan] Sugar was hell bent on imposing his will on other people's lives and careers without giving a second thought to their true views or feelings. There were only two sides to an argument with Sugar – his and the wrong one."

**Teddy Sheringham**

"Being chairman of Tottenham was like having diarrhoea."

**Sir Alan Sugar**

**Spurs director:** "The trouble with you is that you think you know all the answers."

**Blanchflower:** "Ah, God love you, you don't even know the questions."

"Where they find some owners now, I don't know. I remember the first guy they brought in at Portsmouth from Saudi Arabia somewhere. He looked like they pulled him off the stall outside. He looked like the only Arab who didn't have oil in his garden."
**Harry Redknapp**

"I feel like the guy who shot Bambi. I'm not an egotistical loony."
**Alan Sugar on the fans' response to him trying to sack Terry Venables**

"I'm a miserable sod "
**Alan Sugar**

THE FUNNIEST SPURS QUOTES... EVER!

"There's no chance of Sol [Campbell] leaving for Arsenal. He's a Spurs fan and there's not a hope in hell of him playing in an Arsenal shirt."
**David Buchler, Spurs chairman**

"[Alan Sugar] knew nothing about football, but it's often the ones who think they know the game are the problem."
**Gerry Francis**

"We looked all around Europe for people with any credentials, but it is a fact that anyone who is any good was already tied up with a job."
**Alan Sugar not exactly singing the praises of new manager Christian Gross**

"I don't think the fans are too worried whether it's Tom Smith from Bury or Mussolini from Italy... as long as the team's doing well."
**David Pleat on the new Spurs manager**

"When I took over, football was not fashionable. Going into the bank and asking for money was like asking a rabbi to eat a bacon sandwich. Now the banks are queuing up to lend."
**Alan Sugar on the changing face of football**

"I know more about schmaltz herring than I do about football."
**Alan Sugar to then-chairman Irving Scholar before taking over in 1991**

**THE FUNNIEST SPURS QUOTES... EVER!**

Printed in Poland
by Amazon Fulfillment
Poland Sp. z o.o., Wrocław

52272867R00074